STOP BULLYING
Pocketbook
2nd edition

By Michele Elliott

Cartoons:
Phil Hailstone

060037

Published by:

Teachers' Pocketbooks
Laurel House, Station Approach,
Alresford, Hampshire SO24 9JH, UK
Tel: +44 (0)1962 735573
Fax: +44 (0)1962 733637
E-mail: sales@teacherspocketbooks.co.uk
Website: www.teacherspocketbooks.co.uk

*Teachers' Pocketbooks is an imprint of
Management Pocketbooks Ltd.*

With thanks to Brin Best for his help in
launching the series.

First edition published 2005.
This edition 2010.

ISBN 978 1 906610 26 5

British Library Cataloguing-in-Publication Data.
A catalogue record for this book is available
from the British Library.

Design, typesetting and graphics by Efex Ltd.
Printed in UK.

Contents

Introduction

There is brilliant anti-bullying work going on in schools and that is down to the hard work of teachers. In the past, some people have clung to the idea that bullying was just a necessary part of growing up. Thank goodness those attitudes have gone the way of stuffing children up chimneys and sending them down mines.

However, the paradox is that bullying itself is on the rise and new ways of tormenting victims have grown with the advent of computer technology. Cyber bullying means pupils (and teachers) can be targeted 24 hours a day by unscrupulous and cruel bullies. And once the doctored photographs, nasty comments, lies and websites, etc are online, they seem to go on forever, humiliating their victims on a global scale.

I know how hard it can be to do the hundreds of things expected of us and deal with the bullying of pupils – and perhaps even with being bullied ourselves. That is why I am so pleased that this easy to use, handy Pocketbook includes lots of tried and trusted exercises, practical tips and information to fit into your busy day. The ideas come not only from my 40 years of teaching and running the anti-bullying charity Kidscape, but from all my colleagues out there who have contributed. Thanks to all of you and do let me know if you have any suggestions to share in the next edition.

What Do We Know About Bullying?

 Teacher Tips

 Creating a Bully-free School

 Awareness-raising for Pupils

 Understanding Bullies and Victims

 Helping the Bullied and the Bullies

 Suggestions for Everyone

What Do We Know About Bullying?

Defining bullying

Girls in her class called Sally names, but when she complained she was told that it was only a bit of teasing. How often have you heard that? *'It isn't really bullying – it is only name-calling'*. However, any form of deliberate, hurtful behaviour like name-calling IS bullying, if the bully persists knowing the victim is upset by the taunts.

When discussing bullying with pupils (and perhaps staff) it helps if you agree broadly about what bullying is. Professor Dan Olweus, of the University of Bergen, sets down three main features that are always present:

1. There is deliberate aggression.
2. There is an unequal balance of power.
3. The aggression results in pain and distress.

You could either use this definition as it is or see it as a starting point for your own.

Bullying is repeated intimidation intentionally carried out by a more powerful person or group in order to cause physical and/or emotional hurt.

Types of bullying

Asking pupils for examples of bullying often gets a lively discussion going and gives you an insight into what might be happening out there.   Try priming them with a few ideas:

Physical: Pushing, kicking, hitting, pinching and other forms of violence or threats such as, *'I'll be waiting after school to get you if you don't give me your money now'*

Verbal: Name-calling, sarcasm, spreading nasty rumours, cruel teasing

Emotional: Excluding, tormenting, ridiculing, humiliating, threatening gestures

Racist: Using racist taunts, gestures or graffiti

Sexual: Abusive sexual comments, homophobic slurs or gestures

Cyber or online: Texting hurtful comments, setting up hate websites, phoning a mobile to abuse the victim, posting images and messages to vilify victims

An exercise

Here's an exercise you could suggest if you are working with a group of colleagues (or pupils) and want to discuss and agree on an acceptable definition of bullying.

Find a partner. Each person tells about an incident of bullying they remember from childhood, something that happened to them or to someone else. Allow a few minutes for pairs to exchange information. Starting like this breaks the ice and involves everyone.

Next, ask the group to think about stories or incidents of bullying (including cyber bullying) they are familiar with and to identify the key elements that made these incidents 'bullying'. As the group calls out elements, note them on a flip chart, board or screen. Use the results to try to reach agreement on a definition of your own.

HUMILIATING

HURTFUL

FRIGHTENING

PHYSICAL VIOLENCE

NASTY

AGGRESSIVE

MENTAL ABUSE

PERSISTENT

ABUSIVE

BELITTLING

EXCLUSION

SECRET

OSTRACISING

DELIBERATE

SHAMING

Why does bullying happen?

Watching young children grab toys or thump another child over the head because she or he got in the way, makes us wonder if bullying is just part of human nature. Perhaps it is. We all want what we want when we want it, but we learn to modify our behaviour (some of us) and most of us do not go on to bully others.

Bullying happens for a very simple, basic reason: the bully needs a victim and looks for someone to bully. In 99% of cases, the victim has done absolutely nothing to provoke the bully, except to exist. There are a few children who seem to go out of their way to bother people, but we will discuss them in the section on victims.

Why does it continue?
Because no one steps in to stop it and the bully gains more power until it becomes a big problem affecting lots of students and teachers.

How widespread is bullying?

Most studies show that bullying takes place in all schools to some extent. Even if we do our best to tackle it, we all have to deal with it at some time or other.

If someone tells you, *'There has never been any bullying in our school'*, be suspicious. Either they work in a school with two students who are best friends, or they just do not want to know. One mother rang Kidscape to say that her son had been bullied so badly he attempted suicide. The response from the headteacher was that the boy should 'pull himself together because life is tough'. Fortunately most teachers are enlightened and are doing their best to ensure that bullying is eradicated.

Recent surveys indicate that over 50% of pupils and 15% of teachers have been victims of bullying online. Because of the reach of the internet it seems bullying is not only widespread, but growing insidiously.

Signs of bullying

Children and young people who are being bullied are likely to display classic signs. Their school work may suffer while they themselves may:

- Be upset or secretive when looking at or using their mobile phone or computer
- Appear depressed and/or anxious
- Be fearful of certain places and/or people
- Not eat lunch (they're avoiding the lunchroom, or bullies may have taken their money)
- Write stories or talk about suicide – take it very seriously (see page 21)
- Regularly have books, homework or clothes 'go missing'
- Be frightened of or unwilling to go to school, walk home, take the school bus
- Become aggressive, angry, disruptive and may lash out

These may indicate other problems but try asking directly if the child is being bullied. Report your concerns to other appropriate staff.

Bullying matters because...

If you meet resistance to the idea that stopping bullying is important, try a few facts:

- Several young people commit suicide every year because of it
- Over half of the victims of bullying who come to Kidscape's ZAP anti-bullying assertiveness courses (see page 92) have attempted suicide
- Children who are being bullied cannot concentrate on their school work – they can only think about how to get away from their tormentors
- Bullies who are not stopped are four times more likely to end up in prison than people who are not bullies
- Victims and bullies suffer from low self-esteem and lack confidence
- Teachers leave the profession because they are bullied

There are many more reasons, but suffice to say that bullying has a long-lasting negative effect on everyone involved, not least on teachers who have to deal with it.

Teachers are bullied too

We know that some teachers have left the profession because of bullying by pupils and parents – and sometimes even by other staff. In March 2009, a survey conducted by the Association of Teachers and Lecturers and Teacher Support Network found that 15% of teachers have also been victims of cyber bullying. There have been:

- Hate websites
- False accusations online of sexual abuse
- Fake profiles created with digitally changed photographs and untrue defamatory statements
- Online campaigns to sack perfectly competent teachers
- Postings on YouTube ridiculing teachers, etc

Teachers should follow the same advice as pupils (see page 32) by keeping records as evidence: noting time, date and the site; taking copies and photographs; notifying the servers and telling school authorities. Students need to be told in the guidelines about bullying that the police will be called to investigate any such incidents and that the school has a zero tolerance policy.

How bullying thrives

Bullying comes into our lives as teachers all too frequently. We may not be able to stop what is happening to the bully at home or outside our school gates, but within our classrooms bullying thrives when:

- Adults sit back, throw up their hands and say nothing can be done
- Bullying is considered a normal or even essential part of growing up
- Children or young people have too much power over other children
- There is no private way for victims to get help
- Telling is discouraged
- There is no effective anti-bullying policy
- There are no consequences when bullying is discovered
- Victims are blamed for being 'too nice' or 'not tough enough'
- Teachers and staff are afraid of the bully or are being bullied themselves
- Teachers and staff are not backed up when trying to tackle bullying
- Children have unsupervised access to computers

Teachers getting it right

Headteachers and staff who have managed to stop or drastically reduce bullying have several things in common:

- They have an anti-bullying policy that states, 'this is a telling school' and, 'bullying of any kind is not tolerated'
- They ensure the pupils take in this message through assemblies, classroom work, computer use, contracts and posters
- They involve students in writing anti-bullying codes
- They conduct surveys to find out where, when and how bullying is occurring
- They inform parents that bullying will not be tolerated

Go teachers!

Also they:

- Ensure the consequences for bad behaviour and rewards for good behaviour are clear, known by all and enforced
- Ensure something is done to stop the bullying and to protect victims
- Give pupils access to help privately, so the victims can tell in safety
- Talk about anti-bullying strategies in lessons and assemblies
- Train all staff to recognise signs and symptoms of bullying
- Have the proverbial 'eyes in the back of their heads'
- Monitor computer use in classroom

Immediate consequences of bullying

When bullying occurs, there are usually immediate consequences.
Victims may:

- Lose confidence and self-esteem
- Become withdrawn and nervous
- Be unable to concentrate
- Begin to do badly in their academic work
- Truant, develop school phobia, attempt suicide
- Misbehave at home, causing tension within their families
- Be fearful of using computers, mobile phones

Consequences for bullies

It won't surprise you to know that letting bullies off leads to all kinds of negatives. Other children learn that using aggression/violence is a successful strategy for getting what you want, and as for the bullies, they:

- Realise that they can get away with cruel behaviour, eroding school discipline
- Become divisive as a dominant group – those not in the main group are left out and ignored
- Become more disruptive, eventually testing members of staff to see how far they can push them
- Suffer, as their underlying problems may be masked by aggressive behaviour and go untreated
- Set up hate groups on social networking sites attacking pupils and/or teachers

Long-term consequences of bullying

Kidscape conducted the first retrospective study of 1000 adults who were bullied as children. They said the emotional scars were deep, and that the fear and loneliness they experienced as childhood victims still affected the way they looked at the world.

Adult victims of childhood bullying can suffer from:

- Depression
- Low self-esteem
- Fear of meeting strangers
- Guilt, shame
- Social isolation
- Psychosomatic diseases
- Agoraphobia
- Anxiety/panic attacks
- Exceptional timidity
- Anger

They can also be more susceptible to approaches from cults and other unscrupulous organisations that play on their insecurities.

David, now 22, wrote:
'It was bad enough being beaten, spit on and ostracised, but the worst was all the stuff they put on the internet. They imposed my head on the bodies of animals and porn stars, wrote lies online about me, sent hate emails to my friends supposedly from me. I know these things are still online and I get anxiety attacks even now thinking I will have to explain it all to my adult friends. They nearly ruined my life.'

Jane, aged 29, wrote:
'The bullying from girls in my secondary school was so intimidating that I went around with my head down, desperate not to antagonise them. I never knew why they hated me so much. One day, a man on the street invited me to a free lecture about being assertive. I screwed up my courage and went. Everyone was so friendly and welcoming that I felt wanted for the first time. They told me that I was intelligent and exactly the kind of person to take their course. I eventually got sucked into what I now know was a cult. Looking back, I realise that it was my lack of confidence caused by the bullying that made me a perfect target for them. They bullied me into the cult. I am out of it now and getting my life together.'

Suicide and bullying

Suicide as a result of bullying is on the rise throughout the world. In some countries young people are even being arrested after their victim commits suicide. Teachers are devastated when this happens – concerned for both the victim and the bullies and about what, if anything, they could have done to prevent it. What signs should you look out for?

- Losing interest in more things, depressed
- Talking about or writing poems, notes, stories about death and dying
- Appearing to be sad, hopeless, tired, withdrawn, a failure
- Rumours from other children about someone feeling suicidal
- Giving away possessions and suddenly seeming to be content
- Acting irrationally, recklessly, dramatic change in personality or appearance
- Comments such as 'I hate life', 'nothing matters', 'the world would be better off without me'

Young people will exhibit these signs occasionally, but several together could indicate suicidal thoughts. Immediately express your concerns to appropriate staff and get help.

Long-term consequences for bullies

- Uncontrollable, aggressive behaviour/psychiatric disorders
- Criminal convictions/alcohol abuse
- Abuse of children and partners
- Relationship breakdowns
- Employment problems

One study found that children who were bullies at age 12 were four times more likely than their peers to have criminal convictions for aggression and violence. The long-term outlook for chronic bullies is poor.

Because bullying is so destructive, we must take positive steps to eradicate it. It is not some inevitable natural phenomenon; we can control it. The following chapter has ideas from lots of teachers who have tried – and often succeeded – in tackling this thorny problem. See which of them are useful for you.

Teacher Tips

Staff concerns

Staff members often feel uncertain, annoyed, and even angry about having to get involved in tackling bullying. They may also be concerned if they themselves are being bullied. This short exercise can help clarify staff worries.

Break into small groups and give each person a copy of the comments on the next page, or make up your own. Each group can choose two or three concerns they think are relevant and discuss them. (The concerns have all been raised in Kidscape workshops, so you can see you're not alone!)

After 10 –15 minutes, come together and discuss your thoughts. You may also want to opt for a few positive solutions so it doesn't turn into just a 'moan session'.

Issues

1. Never mind the children bullying each other, what are we going to do about children, parents or other teachers bullying the teachers?
2. What about bullies on the staff who bully the kids and other staff members?
3. Bullying takes place going to and from school – is that our problem?
4. What about kids who are bullies and have bullies for parents? What happens when we try to stop their kids being bullies?
5. Won't it seem like we've got a real problem with bullying if we start to bring it out in the open? Will we get a reputation as a 'bully school'?
6. How can we deal with cyber bullying?
7. What about kids being driven to suicide?

It's amazing how many legitimate concerns emerge once you start discussing bullying.

What is our role?

Adults affect bullying in three ways:

1. We **permit** it by our lack of concern for victims and by not tackling incidents.
2. We **promote** it by our attitudes and by allowing bullies to get away with it.
3. We **prevent** it by taking action and by challenging bullying whenever it takes place.

Permitting

Bullying is **permitted** by teachers when:

- Victims are ignored or blamed
- We do not listen to what children tell us
- Victims who tell are told to sort it out themselves
- Victims are too scared to tell
- We encourage retaliation
- There are no effective policies or procedures for dealing with bullying
- Bullies know nothing will happen and gain power

Promoting

Bullying is **promoted** by teachers when:

- We are dismissive of what children tell us
- We are aggressive and sarcastic role models
- We humiliate children in front of their peers
- We pick on individuals or roll our eyes when they approach us
- We are impatient with the less able or irritating children
- We are unapproachable and insensitive
- We do not set limits or consequences to bad behaviour
- Classroom management is poor

Preventing

Bullying is **prevented** by teachers when:

- We listen to children and encourage them to tell about bullying
- We are fair
- Differences between individuals are celebrated
- We raise children's self-esteem
- We are assertive, not aggressive, role models
- Anti-bullying policies and procedures are devised and implemented
- We act immediately to stop and condemn bullying, fighting or cruelty
- We make it clear to pupils that there will be consequences for bullying
- We keep records of incidents
- We do not blame victims for being bullied
- We encourage and reward good behaviour

Attitudes

If we are serious about wanting to tackle bullying in our schools, we have to examine our own attitudes first. When staff display bullying behaviour, no matter how good our school's anti-bullying policy is, pupils will get the message that bullying is acceptable.

Professor Dan Olweus (see page 6) concludes:

> '*The attitudes, routines, and behaviours of the school personnel, particularly those of the teachers, are **decisive factors** in preventing and controlling bullying activities, as well as in redirecting such behaviours into more socially acceptable channels.*'

I met and worked with Dan in Norway, where he has managed almost to eradicate bullying. I was impressed by how much of what he said turned out to be true.

Cyber bullying

Cyber bullying needs its own page because it's the fastest-growing type of bullying, making victims vulnerable 24 hours a day, 7 days a week. Nowhere is safe. Cyber bullying is ongoing, insidious and follows the victims, pupils or teachers, wherever they go. It includes:

- Nasty comments on Facebook for all to see
- Embarrassing and made-up photos posted on social networks
- Hate websites and blogs set up to vilify the victim
- Creating fake user accounts pretending to be a friend of the victims, then publicly dumping them saying they are ugly, stupid and disgusting
- Sending horrible text messages and images to the victim and everyone else
- Using chat rooms, instant messaging and gaming areas to harass victims

Since young people get alerts and they check constantly for messages, this kind of bullying spreads like wildfire. It is instant and nowhere is safe for the victims. It is also done from a distance so many of the bullies can hide their nefarious deeds easier.

Cyber bullying – what to do

- Block and report – use the features available online to block messages. Keep copies and report the abuse to the server. Teachers and school administration should ask for IT support and the latest software
- Don't reply or retaliate – you might be accused of being part of the problem
- Don't forward – resist sending on nasty photos or messages. The bully is using you and you could get into trouble
- Think how you would feel – be careful about what you say or post online
- Threatening behaviour is against the law, that includes online/text threats
- Save all evidence – keep records and copies of messages, photos, websites, texts, online conversations
- Tell someone in authority – that applies if you are a pupil or a teacher on the receiving end of cyber bullying or any bullying
- Do not talk about the cyber bullying to other pupils before reporting it – they may try to intimidate you into keeping quiet
- Make sure that the ways to report cyber bullying are clear to pupils and to staff

Schools designed for bullies

Old buildings with poky rooms and long, dark corridors provide plenty of places where bullies can corner their victims. Outside buildings like bike-sheds are a bully paradise. Although we cannot rebuild our schools, we can ensure that supervision is adequate and we can encourage victims to tell where and when they were bullied in order to pin down likely trouble spots or times.

In one school bullying was rife at break-times so the headteacher moved his office to a room overlooking the playground. Bullying diminished rapidly once the bullies realised their **every move was monitored** by a glance out of the window.

Governors in another school approved the use of a camera that was trained on the playground during breaks. Just knowing that they might be **captured on film** stopped the bullying behaviour almost overnight. **Use a fake camera if your budget is tight**.

Supervision

Adequate supervision of students is very important. Playground supervisors and catering staff should be involved in the anti-bullying policy from the beginning; they are well placed to see if bullying continues and to identify both bullies and victims.

Staff attitudes, the physical layout of the school and the adequacy of supervision arrangements are all important when devising anti-bullying strategies.

Other factors that can promote bullying are:

- Low staff morale
- High teacher turnover
- Unclear standards of behaviour
- Inconsistent methods of discipline
- Remote and unapproachable staff

Take a look at the 'perfect school for bullies' on the next page. Or you might want to ask your pupils to design one; it can be a real eye opener to what is happening.

A perfect school for bullies

The list opposite is not meant to be exhaustive – everyone will have something to add! It was compiled by Peter Smith and Peter Stephenson, teachers and psychologists who have extensively researched bullying in the UK. One teacher said the list 'perfectly described' his school.

- Unsupervised toilets/bike-sheds
- No space for 'quiet' activities
- Bare, empty, unsupervised playground
- Not enough equipment in gyms and labs
- Areas where staff never go
- Whole school queueing at once for meals
- Old buildings with dark, secluded corners
- Staff never around – always in staffroom
- Staff too busy to notice incidents
- Unsupervised meal queues
- Narrow, dark corridors
- Crowded locker rooms
- Everyone arriving and leaving at once
- Long changeovers between lessons
- Teachers being late/leaving class early
- Chaotic classrooms
- Teachers who point/shout/poke
- Teachers who use sarcasm as a weapon
- No support for pupils with special needs
- No support for new pupils
- Staff who bully
- Reporting bullying seen as 'telling tales'
- No clear procedures for dealing with bullying
- General lack of supervision and discipline

Immediate action

Successful intervention is at the heart of an effective whole school anti-bullying strategy. Reporting incidents is also vital: all students must understand that if they bully, they will be reported and all reports will be followed up.

It is important to deal with the immediate fall-out from the bullying incident as quickly as possible, given all the other constraints on staff time. Delay can be interpreted as hesitation on the part of the staff and this can undermine the positive message that bullying will not be tolerated.

Try to keep the investigation simple and not get too bogged down in details. You will need to listen to both sides of the story or you may miss the problems that each side has or, worse, be seen as refusing to be impartial.

Just and only

'Just' and 'only' are key words often used by bullies to defend their behaviour. They are used to diminish the seriousness of whatever has happened.

Examples:
'I **only** pushed her'
'I **just** hit him once'
'We were **only** teasing'

From the victims' viewpoint, they were pushed, or hit – 'only' and 'just' are irrelevant.

Try banning the words 'only' and 'just' from all explanations. So, change *'I only pushed her'*; *'I just kicked her once'*, to *'I pushed her'*; *'I kicked her once.'*

Game, joke, accident

Teachers are often told, by way of excuse, 'It was a game', or 'It was a joke', or 'It was an accident'. So, try asking these questions to clarify what you are told:

'It was a game'.
Did everyone join in? Was anybody left out? Did they want to be left out? If it really was a game, then everyone should have been happy to play and those not playing would have chosen not to join in.

'It was a joke'.
Was everyone laughing? Did everyone find it funny? If it really was a joke, as alleged, then everyone should be amused.

'It was an accident'.
Has someone gone to fetch help? Has anyone apologised? Is anyone comforting the person who has been hurt? This is what happens after a real accident. If it's not happening, then whatever happened was not 'an accident'.

No excuses

Sometimes excuses can be bizarre: one mother, when told her daughter had been fighting other girls, said, *'I'm sure she hit them in a nice way.'*

Borrowing is often used as a way to excuse bullying. One school makes children borrow only from staff and keeps records.

The object of not accepting these lame excuses is to get the bullies to own up to what they have done and not to rationalise away the pain they have caused others. Otherwise the bullies' behaviour will not change and the excuses will go on and on.

Action plan

The steps on this page and the next are given as a general guide. You will want to include your own particular requirements.

- If you witness bullying, the first step is obviously to stop it and remove the bully, perhaps to a 'time-out' area where they can go and cool off
- Reassure victims that they will be protected. If pupils come forward to tell you about bullying, praise them for telling
- If the victim is hurt, seek medical attention and/or ring parents
- If there are bruises or cuts, it might be useful to take pictures so that later denials of harm can be dealt with quickly
- Ask the bully to think of ways to atone for his/her actions – insist on compensation for items lost, damaged or stolen, the return of items 'borrowed' or stolen, and the repayment of money stolen
- Tell pupils (and teachers) to keep copies and timed/dated records of bullying texts, webpages, blogs etc
- Ensure school has appropriate computer safety software

Action plan

The bully should then apologise to the victim. The bully may not feel genuine remorse; nevertheless, accept even the most grudging apology. Work towards teaching *how to apologise*. We want to teach that hurting people is wrong and that when you hurt someone you acknowledge this to yourself and to the person you have hurt. Saying sorry is the first step towards recognising that bullying behaviour is wrong.

Alternatively, if the bullying involves squabbling or minor incidents between generally well-motivated children, sort the situation out by sitting down and getting them to talk about what happened and why. A round discussion gives everyone a chance to air and resolve any grievances.

I'm sorry

Consequences

You may need to help children who bully to understand that:

- Aggressive, violent, or cruel behaviour is unacceptable and if they act in this way they will face consequences
- If assault or theft is involved, it may be necessary to contact police. (The parents of the victim will need to be consulted – some will not press charges and will not be happy if the police are called)
- Cyber bullying can also result in prosecution

You may want to try **additional consequences**, such as:

- Withdrawal of school journey privilege, or computer time
- Filling in a report, sending a letter home and/or holding a meeting with parents
- Helping the bully discuss his/her actions with a peer mentor

More ideas for consequences

Teachers say these ideas work at least sometimes:

- Assigning a senior pupil to monitor/befriend the bully
- Having the bully assist a member of staff with special tasks at break times
- Keeping bullies in during breaks or having them eat, or work alone
- If the bully is bothering pupils on the way home from school, keeping the bully behind to allow the other children to go home unmolested
- Photographing the bully's actions so he/she can't say, '*I didn't do it*'
- Assigning the bully to extra duties: sorting and stacking books, checking cloakrooms, etc (praise for doing well)
- Ensuring only supervised computer time

One school that had an epidemic of pupils kicking each other, decided that a child caught kicking would have his/her shoes removed for the day and wear slippers instead. They had permission from parents.

Telling off!

I am indebted to many teachers like Eric Jones, who has had years of experience as a Deputy Head and classroom teacher and who calls it as he sees it. He says not to forget that the '*good old fashioned telling-off, done formally, without interruption, and then put on record*' can be very effective.   He warns not to be sarcastic, vengeful or personally insulting, but to state facts about unacceptable behaviour and consequences to actions. '*It should point towards the future, hoping for something better, expecting something better*' and then '*the incident put behind us with the culprit being given a chance to prove him/herself or otherwise*'.

Some of us may be too worried about false accusations to give this a try, but please let me know your best 'Teacher Tips': michele@kidscape.org.uk   In the meantime, delve into the ideas in the next chapter to create that bully-free school.

What Do We Know About Bullying?

 Teacher Tips

 Creating a Bully-free School

 Awareness-raising for Pupils

 Understanding Bullies and Victims

 Helping the Bullied and the Bullies

 Suggestions for Everyone

Creating a Bully-free School

Start with parents

Having absorbed a few tips from other teachers, try the practical step-by-step ways in this chapter to engage parents/carers, survey pupils, set up contracts and review your anti-bullying policy.

The start of the school year is the ideal time to talk with parents about possible problems before they actually arise, so that no one feels defensive. In the first meeting, in the midst of trumpeting your fantastic lunchroom, staff and students, point out that children make mistakes, do nasty things, and that you will need the parents' help all along the way. Gain their trust before any bullying begins.

It is also a good idea to write to parents to let them know about your anti-bullying policy. In the past, the reputation of some schools has suffered as parents have mistakenly assumed that because the school was tackling bullying, it must have a major bullying problem. This is an unfortunate misconception, so a letter setting out the school's anti-bullying policy will clarify the situation, reassure parents and prevent the switchboard lighting up with 100 telephone calls! The most common complaint on the Kidscape helpline is that schools don't tell parents about their anti-bullying policy or strategies nor what consequences there are for bullying.

Contact with home

If you have to contact parents or carers about their child being a bully (always difficult and usually denied vehemently) or a victim, try asking if anything has happened lately:

- Has anything happened which could explain the bullying?
- What do they think is happening at school?
- Is the child bullying or being bullied by anyone at home?
- Is their child receiving or sending bullying messages online or by text?
- Did they know, and how long have they known, about the bullying?
- Have they talked to their child about his/her concerns and worries?
- Have they been approached by the bully's/victim's family? Outcome?
- Has anything like this happened before? How was it resolved?
- Have the parents any ideas for working with you to sort out the problem?

Assure the parents that you will deal with the situation and keep them informed. Give them the advice on the next two pages and they will feel you are trying to help.

Advice for parents of children who are being bullied

- Don't ignore the problem – talk to the teachers and work together
- Encourage your child to talk to you about his/her feelings
- Try not to over-react – it might frighten your child into silence
- Ask your child if he/she has any suggestions that would help
- Find out if your child feels safe and protected at school and online
- Take any threats of suicide or other desperate pleas seriously and seek help – children sometimes go to extremes if they are miserable
- Help your child develop strategies for dealing with and reporting bullying – Kidscape has advice on www.kidscape.org.uk
- Praise your child, tell him/her how much you love and support them
- Try to sort out the bullying at the start, as constructively as possible, with the school
- Encourage your child to develop new interests which might lead to a supportive group of friends – in school and out of school

Advice for parents of children who are bullying

- Calmly ask your child if he/she can explain what has happened and why
- Find out if there are ways you can work together to stop his/her behaviour
- Explain that the bullying must stop – whether it's online, via text or in person
- Explain how frightening the bullying is for the victim and encourage empathy
- Criticise the bullying behaviour, but don't reject your child or label him/her as a 'bully' (*'What you did was wrong'* not *'You're a terrible person or a bully'*)
- Look for good behaviour from your child and praise it
- Tell your child you know he/she can change bullying behaviour and that your child is NOT really a bully. Be confident that your child will change
- Help your child to develop new interests and/or friends away from bullies
- Spend as much time with your child as you can, especially listening to his/her concerns. Sometimes children bully as a way of getting attention
- Make it clear that you do not accept bullying behaviour and there will be consequences such as loss of privileges if the bullying does not stop
- Monitor your child's computer use

Student councils

Having gained the support of parents, now try setting up effective ways to work with pupils.

One way that has worked in many schools is enlisting the support of the student council.   Part of its remit can be to deal with positive ways to tackle bullying. Pupils usually know much more about the bullying situation in a school than the adults, which is hardly surprising. Using their good will and expertise can dramatically cut down the time you have to spend dealing with incidents.

The council can set the tone and help devise, distribute and collate questionnaires about bullying (see the following pages). It can suggest ways to keep children safe and even possible consequences for bullying behaviour. This does not imply draconian solutions.   School councils have opted for a time-out place for the bully to cool off, suggested ways the bully could be more effective in making friends, made sure that victims had a 'buddy' or that new pupils were given mentors. They also have good ideas for stopping cyber bullying.

'Bullying' questionnaire

Work with the student council to
write and oversee a questionnaire/survey
to find out:

- If bullying is taking place
- If pupils are interested or concerned
- Where it is happening
- When it is happening
- Patterns of bullying
- What groups are involved in bullying

Ensure the format allows answers to be
anonymous (see following pages).

How to use the questionnaire

It could be a small group of staff volunteers who work with the pupils to devise a questionnaire. Some schools also include parents in this process, which helps to eliminate any future misunderstandings. Alternatively, you can use or adapt the following questionnaires to save time and your sanity.

It is best if the students fill out their questionnaires anonymously – they will more likely answer honestly. Pupils may be worried that their handwriting will be recognised. To overcome this, the questionnaire could have tick boxes, or be given online; the format will obviously depend upon the age and abilities of children. Some children may need help to fill in the answers, so anonymity may not be possible.

When the findings are summarised, discuss and distribute them to the whole staff, including meals and playground supervisors, and the pupils.

Sample questionnaire for young children

Ask the children to fill in the blanks with drawings or with happy or sad faces or words. You will obviously have to leave more space for drawing than I can include here.

Who makes you happy? Does anyone make you unhappy?

Draw a happy 😊 or a sad 🙁 face to show if you are happy or unhappy in these places:

😊 Playground	😊 Classroom
😊 Toilets	😊 Lunchroom
😊 Coming to school	😊 Going home from school
😊 On my mobile	😊 On my computer

Young person questionnaire

a) Have you ever been bullied in this school? ☑ yes ☐ no

b) When? ☐ now ☑ sometime this year ☐ in the past

c) Did/do you consider the bullying ☐ not bad ☐ worrying ☑ terrible?

d) Was it so bad that you didn't want to go to school? ☐ yes ☐ no

e) Did the bullying ☐ have no effect ☐ some bad effect ☐ terrible effect
☐ make you want to change schools?

f) Is the bullying still happening? ☐ yes ☐ no

g) If the bullying is still happening, where is it occurring? ☐ classroom
☐ halls ☐ during sports ☐ toilet ☐ after school ☐ lunchroom
☐ library ☐ activities ☐ breaktime ☐ everywhere ☐ online

h) How often is the bullying happening? ☐ seldom ☐ once a day
☐ several times a day ☐ once a week ☐ once a month ☐ all the time

i) Is the bullying ☐ physical ☐ verbal ☐ racial ☐ homophobic
☐ sexual ☐ emotional (being ignored etc) ☐ threat
☐ taking possessions ☐ text ☐ email ☐ mobile ☐ website?

j) Do you know anyone who is being bullied, but has not told? ☐ yes ☐ no

k) Are you a ☐ girl ☐ boy?

l) Is the bully (or bullies) ☐ girl ☐ boy ☐ both ☐ a gang ☐ teacher
☐ other member of staff ☐ other?

m) If you were or are being bullied, have you ever told anyone? ☐ yes ☐ no

n) Did the bullying stop when you told? ☐ yes ☐ no

o) Did the bullying become worse because you told? ☐ yes ☐ no

p) Have you ever bullied anyone? ☐ yes ☐ no

q) Are you bullying someone in this school now? ☐ yes ☐ no

r) What should be done about the problem of bullying? (Optional)

School contracts

A carefully devised contract is a good way of ensuring that everybody knows what they can and cannot do. Nobody can say, *'I didn't know it wasn't allowed'*.
If bullying takes place, victims know that they can tell and bullies know that they will not be able to depend on the silence of victims or witnesses for protection.

Contracts are not just imposed arbitrarily upon the student body. They are discussed and amended, and the final version is the result of agreement and compromise.

Why a school contract?

So what are the advantages of a school contract?

- Everybody knows what is acceptable and expected of them
- They provide clear simple guidelines
- They eliminate *'I didn't know it wasn't allowed'* excuse
- Students from different racial and cultural backgrounds are protected
- Sexual harassment and homophobia are outlawed
- They teach pupils how to behave as responsible members of the school
- They involve pupils so that they 'own' it and it reflects their concern

Using the contract

If contracts are printed on coloured paper they are easily visible and retrievable. You may also wish to put a notation on the contract of the year or term it covers. There are a number of ways of using contracts.

- The contract can be distributed to every pupil on paper or online
- Each pupil and their parents can be asked to sign a copy to be kept in the pupil's file
- Copies can be displayed in classrooms, and on your school website
- A copy of the contract can be included in the parents' handbook, or emailed
- It can be read to each class at the beginning of term and to each new pupil

Bullying is obviously not the only issue on the agenda: schedules, rosters, lunch arrangements, anti-racism, equal opportunities, homework policies and all sorts of other things may also need to be displayed. Displaying *only* the anti-bullying policy on the school contract may lead visitors to conclude that bullying is rife! Include a variety of issues, all of which apply to most schools, such as taking responsibility in the school, littering, vandalism, acceptance of others, online safety, etc.

Sample contract designed by 11 year olds

CONTRACT

1. We will not tolerate bullying or harassing of any kind.
2. We will be accepting of all races, religions, cultures and disabilities.
3. If we see anyone being bullied, we will either try to stop it or go for help.
4. We will not allow bullying or harassing going to or from school, whether walking, on the school bus or on public transport.
5. We will allow a quiet area at break for those who do not want to play games.
6. We will use our 'time out' room if we feel angry or under pressure or just need time to calm down or work out what is wrong.
7. We will not litter or draw on school property.
8. We will be kind to others, even if they are not our friends and we will make new students feel welcome.
9. On school journeys we will act in a way which brings credit to our school.
10. We will not take part in cyber bullying and will report it.
11. We will have a discussion group once a week in class to talk about problems.
12. We will support the student council and be nice to teachers. (Good idea!)

Producing an anti-bullying policy

Every school is required by law to have an anti-bullying policy. It may seem like just one more thing to do, but it does make dealing with bullying easier in the long run. When parents, staff and pupils know the policy and what will happen, it often cuts down the hassle when bullying rears its ugly head. You probably already have a policy, but if not, here are some suggestions for starting the ball rolling. You can:

1. Break into small groups to work on one particular phase of the policy.
2. Break into small groups and each come up with a complete policy.
3. Give each group a copy of the Kidscape anti-bullying policy and adapt it.
4. Look at your own anti-bullying policy and accept or revise it.
5. Consider adding a help section with local and national numbers.

Kidscape anti-bullying policy

The Kidscape anti-bullying policy, which has evolved from years of working with schools, appears here and on the next two pages. You can adapt it to your own needs or write your own.

'We are committed to providing a caring, friendly and safe environment for our pupils. Bullying of any kind is unacceptable. If bullying does occur, all pupils should be able to tell and know that incidents will be dealt with promptly and effectively. We are a TELLING school – anyone who knows that bullying is happening is expected to tell.'

What is bullying?

Bullying is the use of aggression with the <u>deliberate</u> intention of hurting another person:

Physical: Pushing, kicking, hitting, pinching and other forms of violence or threats

Verbal: Name-calling, sarcasm, spreading nasty rumours

Emotional: Excluding, tormenting, ridiculing, humiliating, threatening gestures

Racist: Using racist taunts, gestures or graffiti

Sexual: Unwanted contact, abusive sexual comments, homophobic slurs

Cyber/online: Texting or phoning threats, setting up hate websites, chat room misuse

Kidscape anti-bullying policy

Objectives
- All staff, governors, pupils and parents know school anti-bullying policy
- Bullying will not be tolerated and will be dealt with effectively
- Clear procedures for reporting bullying are understood and followed

Procedures and consequences
1. Report bullying incidents to staff.
2. Incidents will be recorded by staff, unless minor and sorted out.
3. Parents should be informed if serious case and asked to discuss the problem.
4. If necessary and appropriate, police will be consulted.
5. Bullying behaviour and threats must be investigated and immediately stopped.
6. An attempt will be made to help bullies change their behaviour.
7. Bullies will apologise and other appropriate consequences may take place.
8. In serious cases, suspension or exclusion will be considered.
9. Whenever possible, the pupils will be reconciled.

You can add local and national helplines or advice centres or specific consequences to your policy. Some schools give a copy to all parents, pupils and staff. Some put it in the school handbook.

Awareness-raising for Pupils

Telling

Getting students to talk about and understand bullying is crucial, so here are a few discussion topics and ideas for pupil involvement. There are more in the 'Suggestions for Everyone' section later.

Ask pupils to discuss when it is right to tell about incidents of bullying.

- Do they think of telling as sneaking, grassing, telling tales?
- Is it right to tell if telling will help another person out of trouble or other difficulties like bullying?
- Is it right to tell if telling means getting other people into trouble?
- Is it right to tell to protect yourself?
- When would it be wrong to tell?

The answers are along the lines that it is never wrong to tell if someone is being bullied or hurt. Not telling means you are colluding with the bullies.

Effective communication

This exercise is especially good for both victims and bullies. It is a confidence builder and needs either two people or one person with a mirror.

1. Face the other person (or the mirror)
2. Think a pleasant thought and relax your face. Smile, if you can
3. Make eye contact, but don't stare – this is not a power contest.
4. State your question or request in a firm, friendly voice – don't shout or whisper
5. Don't beg, plead or demand – say clearly what you mean:
   - *'Would you please help me with my maths? I don't understand this'*
   - *'Would you like go to the cinema this Saturday?'*
   - *'Go away and leave me alone'*
6. End the conversation when you are ready:
   - *'Got to get to class. See you'*
   - *'You've been a big help. Thanks. 'Bye'*
   - *'We'll just have to agree to disagree'*

'I am proud that ...'

To help bullies and victims express pride about something they have done.

I am proud that ...

I tried very hard to ....

I did well in ....

I did not ....

I am good at ....

I helped ....

I always ....

I have improved at ....

I will become ....

My greatest achievement is ....

My most exciting ambition is to ....

Design a flag or coat of arms using some of your 'proud' statements.
Make an 'I am proud' collage with pictures or your own drawings.

Put downs

Ask all pupils to think of all the 'put down' comments people make. Write them on the board or flipchart and discuss how they make people feel. Some examples:

Go back where you came from

You're stupid

Why did you do it that way?

Get that shirt from Oxfam?

Too bad about the face

That's gay

Like your hair – NOT

Look who's escaped from the zoo

Also ask them to think of gestures or facial expressions that are 'put downs' such as:

• Holding your nose • Making monkey-like gestures and noises • Rolling your eyes

Ask pupils to spend some time observing and listing comments, gestures and facial expression that are 'put downs'. Discuss how often we use these expressions and then compile a 'build up' rather than a 'put down' list, eg: *That was a good try, well done, never mind,* etc.

Plan of action

Children caught up in bullying benefit from working out how to take control of themselves and to think about where they are going. It might be done in steps:

1. **Learn about yourself**. Am I happy with the way things are going? If not, what can I do to change things?
2. **I'm responsible**. If I am doing something to make myself or others unhappy, then it is my responsibility to change.
3. **What can I do?** What will happen if I continue on this path? What choices do I have? Make a list. What one thing can I work on today/this week?
4. **Plan it out**. What will I do/say when I see the person I am bullying or what will I do/say if I see the person who is bullying me? How will I change this relationship? Write it down, step by step.
5. **Evaluate**. What else could you have done? Did what you do help the situation or make it worse? What will you try next? Use the following exercise, 'A Good Week', to help you evaluate.

A good week

For pupils who are trying to overcome a victim mentality or bullying others (or a combination of both) this is a way to self-evaluate progress.

1. What is the nicest thing that happened to you this week? ....

2. What was the worst thing that happened? ....

3. What was the best thing you did for (or said to) someone? ....

4. What was the best thing you did for yourself? ....

5. Name one thing you changed ....

6. What did you learn about yourself? ....

7. How could this week have been improved? ....

8. My goal for next week is ....

Learn what you live

Give pupils a copy of this poem to discuss. Then follow up with the activity on page 103.

Children Learn What They Live by *Dorothy Law Nolte*
(author approved shortened version)

If children live with criticism, they learn to condemn.
If children live with hostility, they learn to fight.
If children live with ridicule, they learn to be shy.
If children live with shame, they learn to feel guilty.
If children live with encouragement, they learn confidence.
If children live with tolerance, they learn patience.
If children live with praise, they learn appreciation.
If children live with acceptance, they learn to love.
If children live with approval, they learn to like themselves.
If children live with honesty, they learn truthfulness.
If children live with security, they learn to have faith in themselves and in those about them.
If children live with friendliness, they learn that the world is a nice place in which to live.

Adapted from the book *Children Learn What They Live* ©1998 by Dorothy Law Nolte and Rachel Harris
The poem 'Children Learn What They Live' on page vi ©1972 by Dorothy Law Nolte
Used by permission of Workman Publishing Co., New York. All Rights Reserved

What bullying teaches

The poem on the previous page and this activity can lead to insightful group discussion, or personal intervention with one pupil to help them understand the harm of bullying.

Bullying teaches us:

If a child is bullied at home, he/she learns

If a child is bullied by other children, he/she learns

If a child is labelled as a bully, he/she learns

If a child bullies others, he/she learns

If a child asks for help and no one does anything, he/she learns

If a child is told he/she is stupid, he/she learns

If a child is not stopped from bullying, he/she learns

If a child tells about bullying and it gets worse, he/she learns

If a child has a teacher who is a bully, he/she learns

If bullying goes on and other children see it, they learn

If bullying is not stopped, we all learn

Making friends

Although we ask children to become friends, we seldom help them to think of how to go about it. Bullying is sometimes the result of misguided attempts by children to become part of a group or to approach someone to become a friend. Ask pupils working in small groups to discuss ways to make friends and come up with a list of ten ideas. The suggestions here were compiled by a group of 13 year olds:

- Show an interest in what people do
- Be complimentary without going overboard
- Have a pleasant expression on your face
- Offer to help
- Be welcoming to new students
- Bring something interesting to do
- Be fair

- Laugh at people's jokes
- Be kind
- Ask to join in
- Invite people to do activities
- Be willing to share
- Be amusing/tell jokes
- Organise games or activities

Ways NOT to make friends

Using the same method, ask pupils to think about behaviour that is likely to STOP them from making friends. One group thought of the following:

- Being bossy and sarcastic
- Telling others they are doing things wrong
- Talking about yourself all the time
- Talking about other students behind their backs
- Being too intense or serious all the time
- Bullying
- Bragging
- Being negative
- Lying or cheating
- Moaning all the time

Write a paper about an imaginary new student trying to make friends in your school. What obstacles might she encounter? How could you help?

Who can I turn to?

To help children think about who they would turn to for help.

Start with a circle in the middle of the page in which the child writes SELF. Then draw as many 'legs' off the circle as possible. Ask the child to label each leg with the name of a person or organisation from whom they can get help and support or comfort (eg mum, dad, gran, ChildLine, doctor, police, teachers, religious leaders, siblings, dog, neighbour, uncle, Samaritans, Kidscape, etc).

The activities in this chapter were designed mainly for bullies and victims. The next chapter is a smorgasbord for all pupils, with ideas for setting up peer support schemes and teaching positive assertiveness skills and activities to reinforce your anti-bullying ethos.

Suggestions for Everyone

Peer support schemes

The activities in this section have been road tested by teachers of primary, secondary and special needs pupils. You will know best which ones are suited to the children you teach.

'Peer support' is an umbrella term for support schemes giving pupils a chance to share concerns and explore their own solutions. They build on students' natural willingness to seek out their peers when they are experiencing problems, and on their ability to act in a genuine, empathic way toward one another.

Peer support can have a positive influence on the emotional climate of a school. Creating a framework in which pupils can support each other recognises the vital role they can play in making positive changes in their own lives and those of their peers. These schemes can dramatically reduce bullying.

Peer support options

The model chosen should be clearly defined, and the role and responsibilities should be understood and supported by the whole school community.

Peer listeners provide a confidential service as active listeners and facilitators, offering a safe place for pupils to share their concerns and to explore solutions.

Peer mediators trained in conflict resolution strategies may act as intermediaries in response to bullying situations.

Peer mentors are often given a specific focus, such as acting as a befriender to pupils in a new school or as a support for pupils who are vulnerable.

Whichever approach you adopt, it should be compatible with policies and procedures that address issues such as anti-bullying, child protection, confidentiality, record-keeping and equal opportunities.

Peer support – a whole school approach

Peer supporters will require ongoing help and supervision and need active commitment from more than one member of staff.

- Set clear criteria for selecting those who are to be peer supporters

- Peer supporters should receive appropriate and ongoing training. Links with other schools using the same model have proved useful

- Peer support schemes should be monitored and evaluated regularly to ensure that objectives are being met and the pupils feel supported

- Issues such as establishing a rolling training programme, securing space, and allowing time for key staff to liaise with local and national support agencies should also be considered

Peer supporters/mentors

Mentors are not counsellors and are not equipped to deal with suicidal peers, drug problems, abusive families, etc. These situations require professional help and, if handled incorrectly, could lead to a student harming themselves or others. In talking about bullying, it is inevitable that other issues will arise. Peer supporters/mentors and supervisors need to decide on priorities and how to get this information to pupils, parents and staff.

- Which problems will students deal with and which need to go to supervisors?
- What is the purpose of the programme and how will you let the school population, including parents, know about it?
- Where and when will the mentoring/help take place?
- How will the supporters be chosen?
- Who will train the supporters and the supervisors?

Peer supporters can be extremely effective in fostering a positive influence, creating a welcoming, friendly and cooperative atmosphere in schools. It is worth the effort.

Steps to peer support

1. Decide which kind of peer support scheme suits you and your school.
2. Decide which staff members, including a coordinator, will be responsible.
3. Research possible training courses and resources.
4. Decide your criteria for the peer supporters – age, background, personality.
5. Interview and recruit potential peer supporters.
6. Either bring in a training course or, if you feel confident, run it yourself.
7. Start with a small (one year group) peer support team and monitor carefully.
8. Evaluate and roll the programme out, if you are ready.
9. Continuously monitor and liaise with other schools.
10. Have your peer supporters try the exercises and ideas in this book.

Teaching assertiveness skills

Chronic victims and timid or shy children may have poor social skills and might not know how to ask for what they want. Aggressive or boisterous children may just take what they want, or might ask roughly or aggressively. Those in between can always use a top-up on positive ways to behave – can't we all?

It is, therefore, a good idea to do some assertiveness training exercises with the whole class. Assertiveness training teaches all children acceptable ways of behaving. If you are wondering where you will get the time to do this, perhaps you can enlist the help of a parent to help during break time or after school, if necessary.

Making a request

1. **Be clear about what you want**
2. **Make your request short,** eg *'That is my pencil. Give it back please'.*
3. **Plan and practise** even if you just go over the request in your own mind. You have to decide what you are going to say and then stick to it.

Ask pupils to work in pairs. You may wish to give them a list of requests to practise or have them make up their own. Ask pupils to take turns making a simple, assertive request, such as:

'I don't want to walk home that way – let's go a different way.'
'I will not give you my homework to copy.'
'I would like you to move, please.'
'I am listening to that music – please don't change it.'
'That is my book – please give it to me.'
'Please return my jacket now.'
'I don't want to loan you my watch.'

Responding to demands

When a bully makes a demand, it is often difficult for children and young people to know what to say. Try practising responses. Ask the children to divide into pairs, one member to play the bully and the other the victim (switching roles frequently). Encourage them to come up with creative responses, but not inflammatory ones:

'Got any sweets on you?'
'Yes, but they're horrible. My dog licked them.'

'Lend us your homework.'
'OK, but the teacher has already seen it this morning.'

'Lend us dinner money.'
'No borrowing – why not get it from the secretary?'

'We'll be waiting for you after school.'
'OK, let's arrange it with the teacher.'

'You've got my book in your bag – let me have it.'
'Your book is not in my bag.'

Saying no

If you are asked to do something that is wrong or makes you uncomfortable, say no. Be kind but firm. Don't get side-tracked into apologising for your decision or justifying it. Don't make excuses. Keep your body assertive, keep good eye-contact and don't giggle.

Work in pairs (pupils or teachers) and try the following or make up your own:

'No, I don't want to leave right now. But you can go – I'll catch up later.'
'No, I don't like that.'
'No, there is no way I can do that.'
'No, leave me alone, please. I don't want to do that now.'
'No, it is my book and I need it. Maybe I can help you find one.'
'No, it just isn't possible for me to go with you. I have too much work to do.'
'No, you cannot have my chocolate – anyway it fell on the floor.'
'No, I cannot lend you any money. I've only got enough for the bus.'

Shouting no

Teach pupils to shout 'NO' as loudly as they can if they are in trouble or danger. The shout should come from the stomach and sound like a fog horn. Practise with the students (and among staff, it's invigorating). Can be used on difficult colleagues…

Say, 'At the count of three I want you to shout No – One, two, three NOOOOOO!' Good way to wake up a class (and your neighbours – better let them know if this is going to happen). Practise until it becomes an automatic response to danger. I used it when someone tried to mug me and it startled him, allowing me to escape.

Scratched CD

In this exercise, practise saying the same thing over and over again like a scratched CD. This can be used if someone is trying to get round you or not listening.
Ask the children to divide into pairs – one child to be 'A' and the other to be 'B'.

A has a new bicycle. B wants to borrow it. A doesn't want anyone to play with the new bike. B keeps trying to get the bike from A. Give the children a minute in which B keeps asking for the bike, and A keeps saying, 'No'. B can try hard to convince A.

At the end of a minute, ask if any of the Bs got the bike? What reasons were given for wanting to borrow the bike? Was it hard for the As to keep saying no?

Repeat the exercise, but this time have A try to borrow B's new football or mobile.

Fogging

If we respond to insults with more insults, it builds up. Instead we can 'fog'. Fogging swallows up insults like a great fog-bank swallows sights and sounds. You respond to insults by saying nothing or by making a short, bland comment: *'Really?'*; *'It could be'*; *'perhaps you're right'*.

This exercise can be done either working in pairs or in a circle. If you work in a circle, you can control the exercise by letting the children or young people send 'insults' to you while you 'fog' them. Make sure that the ground rules are clear – this isn't a contest about who can come up with the most horrible insult.

If working in pairs, suggest that each pair has something impersonal to insult, such as a pencil or a book:

'That is a dumb book.'   *'That book is written by an idiot.'*
'That is such an ugly pencil.' *'That pencil is an insult to the human race.'*

Everyone is valuable

This should be a fun, rewarding activity. The aim is for pupils to say good things about one another and to see good things about themselves. The rule is: anything written must be positive.

Each person puts their own name at the top of a piece of paper. The papers are then passed on and at each subsequent person a brief comment is added, highlighting the value of the person whose name is at the top. Everyone gets back their own piece of paper with compliments on it. Alternatively, you can tape paper to everyone's back and write comments on that, which works if pupils feel comfortable with being touched on their backs.

Needless to say, there is no deliberate attempt to know who said what about whom. (Children on Kidscape's ZAP assertiveness courses (see page 92) love this exercise and keep their papers to reread – good for egos.)

Balloon debate

This simple and popular game is known as a balloon debate. It highlights the value of individuals. Several people adopt characters, people they know a little about (historical figures, current world figures, or representatives from sport, entertainment, their religion, etc.) and the remainder of the group act as audience.

There follows a brief debate set up by whoever is in the chair. These people are in a hot-air balloon but the balloon is losing height and will crash. Only one of them (or two, or three, or however many suits the circumstances) can stay; the others must be jettisoned overboard. They each make a case for themselves to be saved, citing their value to society, contribution to history or whatever. They do not rubbish other travellers, simply make their own case. When each has stated their case, the audience is asked to vote and the person generating most votes is the one who remains on board! Remind voters they are voting for the character, not the person.

Cornucopia

To give us beleaguered teachers some quick ideas to use in a pinch:

- **Body outline** – For younger children. Ask them to lie down on a large piece of paper (rolls of heavy lining paper from a DIY shop are quite cheap) and trace an outline of their bodies. Ask the children to cut out their outline and colour it in. Use Post-it® notes on which to write about each child and attach it to the outline. Change the message as often as possible – the children will be delighted

- **Perfect school** – Ask pupils to design a perfect school in which everyone is happy and there is no bullying. (The opposite of the exercise on page 35)

- **Millionaire** – Tell pupils they have each inherited £1,000,000, of which they must use 90% to eradicate bullying. After they have stopped all bullying, they can then use the remaining 10% of the money for themselves and must use that 10% to make their own lives happier. What will they do?

Cornucopia

- **Bully Pack** – Ask pupils to write a story about a young person who finds that he/she is being pulled into a bully pack and being pressured to start bullying a person they have been friends with in the past. Ask them to write about what the character might be thinking and feeling and how he/she resolves the problem. Use as a springboard to discuss resisting peer pressure and cyber bullying

- **Victim viewpoint** – After the students have completed the exercise above, ask them to write the same story from the viewpoint of the victim. He/she will be confused, frightened and worried, especially when one of her/his friends joins in the bullying. Include cyber bullying

Cornucopia

- **Bulletin board** – Ask older pupils to look for references to bullying, including racist attacks or attacks on gay or lesbian people or incidents of suicide or suicide attempts attributed to bullying in the press. Use these stories to create a bulletin board and to discuss bullying

- **Mural** – Ask younger children to co-operate on drawing and decorating a class mural. On one panel draw a playground where bullying is happening and on another panel a playground where everyone is having a good time and where there is no bullying. Discuss your own playground and think of ways that could make it like the 'no bullying' panel

That's all the pages the publishers would let me have, but I hope I have given you a taste of how to tackle bullying. You must be the kind of teacher we all want for our children because you were interested enough to read this book and to try to stop bullying in your school. As a fellow teacher, I thank you for that. You probably have great ideas and have tried other techniques that work. I really would like to hear from you: michele@kidscape.org.uk

Websites

The following organisations have a good selection of resources and link to other useful groups. Most include cyber bullying advice and information:

Kidscape	**www.kidscape.org.uk**
Andrea Adams Trust (Workplace Bullying)	**www.andreaadamstrust.org**
Anti-Bullying Network (Racist Bullying)	**www.antibullying.net/racistinfo**
Bullying UK	**www.bullying.co.uk**
Childnet International	**www.childnet-int.org**
Dept for Education	**www.education.gov.uk**
Joint Action Against Homophobic Bullying	**www.intercomtrust.org.uk**
Stonewall (Homophobic Bullying)	**www.stonewall.org.uk**
Stop Cyber bullying (USA Gov)	**www.stopbullyingnow.hrsa.gov**
Lisa's no Pizza	**www.stopbullying.org**

Books and other resources

Other books about bullying by Michele Elliott. (Available from Kidscape, 2 Grosvenor Gardens, London SW1W 0DH, or download information from the website on page 125)

How to Stop Bullying: A Kidscape Training Guide
Bullying: A Practical Guide to Coping for Schools
Bully Free Activities for 15-20 year olds
Bully Wise Guide For 10-16 year olds
Beat The Bullies – Willow Street Kids For 7-11 year olds
101 Ways to Deal with Bullying: A Guide for Parents

Kidscape DVD
Bully Free – based on ZAP Assertiveness Courses for 9-16 year olds
It Shouldn't Happen – for primary aged children

Leaflets:
Preventing Racist Bullying   ***You Can Beat Bullying***   ***Don't Bully Me***
Stop Bullying   ***Preventing Bullying***

About the author

Michele Elliott

Michele is a teacher, psychologist with 40 years' experience, and the founder of the children's charity KIDSCAPE. She is considered to be the UK's foremost expert on prevention of bullying, having pioneered the first research and books on the subject in 1984. Since then she has written 23 books on subjects including bullying, abuse and parenting. She regularly contributes articles and comments to national newspapers, radio and television, as well as to professional journals.

Michele works with the Home Office, the Department for Education, the Department of Health, the World Health Organisation, charities and other agencies, and consults with numerous committees and enquiries. She is a Winston Churchill Fellow and has been awarded an OBE for her work.

Married to a 30 years+ veteran teacher of 13 year olds and the mother of two sons, Michele describes herself as a 'demented, elderly mother and teacher'. Contact her on michele@kidscape.org.uk.

Order form

Your details

Name _____

Position _____

School _____

Address _____

_____

_____

Telephone _____

Fax _____

E-mail _____

VAT No. (EC only) _____

Your Order Ref _____

Please send me:

No. copies

Stop Bullying _____ Pocketbook ☐

_____ Pocketbook ☐

_____ Pocketbook ☐

_____ Pocketbook ☐

Order by Post

Teachers' Pocketbooks
Laurel House, Station Approach
Alresford, Hants. SO24 9JH UK

Order by Phone, Fax or Internet
Telephone: +44 (0)1962 735573
Facsimile: +44 (0)1962 733637
E-mail: sales@teacherspocketbooks.co.uk
Web: www.teacherspocketbooks.co.uk

Customers in USA should contact:
2427 Bond Street, University Park, IL 60466
Tel: 866 620 6944   Facsimile: 708 534 7803
E-mail: mp.orders@ware-pak.com
Web: www.managementpocketbooks.com